J 001 707

P9-CER-199

TEAM SPIRIT ®

SMART BOOKS FOR YOUNG FANS

THE BOSTON RED SOX

BY

MARK STEWART

NORWOOD HOUSE PRESS

CHICAGO, ILLINOIS

Norwood House Press
P.O. Box 316598
Chicago, Illinois 60631

For information regarding Norwood House Press, please visit our website at:
www.norwoodhousepress.com or call 866-565-2900.

All photos courtesy of Getty Images except the following:
SportsChrome (4, 10, 11, 18), Recruit (6), F.W. Rueckheim & Brother (7 both),
Topps, Inc. (9, 35 top left, 36, 37, 42 both), Tom DiPace (14), Golden Press (15), Author's Collection (16, 33),
Black Book Partners Archives (21, 22, 25, 28, 35 bottom & top right, 38, 39, 40, 43 bottom left & right),
Fan Craze (34 bottom left, 41), Gum, Inc. (34 top), Exhibit Supply Co. (43 top),
SSPC, Ltd. (45), Matt Richman (48).
Cover Photo: SportsChrome

The memorabilia and artifacts pictured in this book are presented for educational and informational purposes,
and come from the collection of the author.

Editor: Mike Kennedy
Designer: Ron Jaffe
Project Management: Black Book Partners, LLC.
Special thanks to Topps, Inc.

Library of Congress Cataloging-in-Publication Data

Stewart, Mark, 1960-
  The Boston Red Sox / by Mark Stewart. -- Library ed.
    p. cm. -- (Team spirit)
  Includes bibliographical references and index.
  Summary: "A Team Spirit Baseball edition featuring the Boston Red Sox that
chronicles the history and accomplishments of the team. Includes access to
the Team Spirit website, which provides additional information, updates and
photos"--Provided by publisher.
  ISBN 978-1-59953-475-6 (library : alk. paper) -- ISBN 978-1-60357-355-9
(ebook) 1. Boston Red Sox (Baseball team)--History--Juvenile literature.
I. Title.
  GV875.B62S74 2012
  796.357'640974461--dc23
                                            2011048464

Manufactured in the United States of America in North Mankato, Minnesota.
196N—012012

COVER PHOTO: The Red Sox celebrate a win on their way to their 2007 championship.

TABLE OF CONTENTS

ABOUT OUR GLOSSARY

In this book, there may be several words that you are reading for the first time. Some are sports words, some are new vocabulary words, and some are familiar words that are used in an unusual way. All of these words are defined on page 46. Throughout the book, sports words appear in **bold type**. Regular vocabulary words appear in ***bold italic type***.

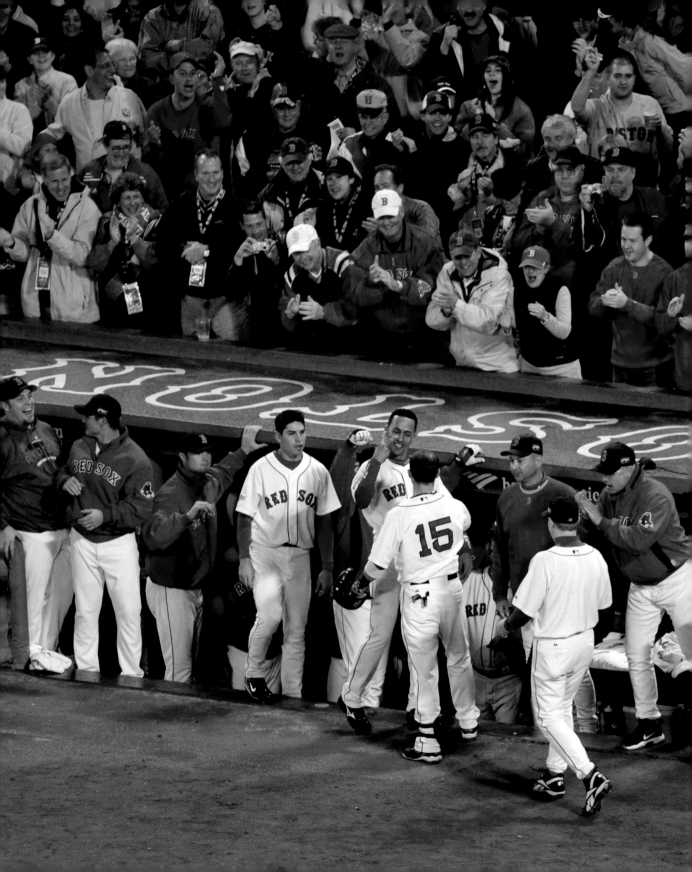

MEET THE RED SOX

When you play for the Boston Red Sox, it doesn't take long to realize that you are part of something big. The team has millions of fans all over its home state of Massachusetts. The Red Sox also are the "home team" for Maine, New Hampshire, Vermont, Rhode Island, and parts of Connecticut and New York.

The Red Sox are part of a long *tradition*—and also a part of American sports history. That is why so many players dream of wearing the Boston uniform. This is true even for those who grew up thousands of miles away.

This book tells the story of the Red Sox. They are one of the best-known and most-loved sports teams in the world. Even in defeat, there has always been something special about the Red Sox. Doing the impossible is what drives the team and its fans.

Red Sox fans cheer for Dustin Pedroia as he returns to the dugout. Pedroia's hard work and skill made him an instant favorite in Boston.

GLORY DAYS

The history of baseball in Boston stretches back to the 1800s. The city has been home to winning teams since the 1870s. In 1901, the **American League (AL)** played its first season. It placed a team in Boston to compete with the **National League (NL)** club that already played there. The new team tried a couple of different names before settling on Red Sox around 1908.

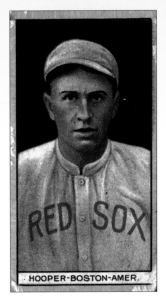

HOOPER-BOSTON-AMER.

By then Boston had already won the **pennant** twice, in 1903 and 1904. The club was successful because it convinced many NL stars to join the team. Players such as Jimmy Collins, Bill Dineen, Cy Young, Chick Stahl, and Buck Freeman were well known to Boston baseball fans. In fact, all of them had played for the city's NL team in 1900!

From 1912 to 1918, the Red Sox won the AL pennant and the **World Series** four times. These teams were among the greatest in history. Boston's incredible pitching staff included Joe Wood, Rube Foster, Ernie Shore,

LEFT: Harry Hooper was the finest outfielder of his time.   **RIGHT**: Tris Speaker and Joe Wood were stars of the team that won four pennants from 1912 to1918.

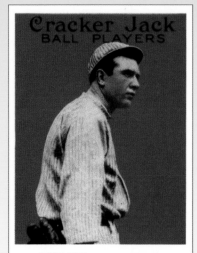

SPEAKER, Boston - Americans

Dutch Leonard, Carl Mays, Joe Bush, and Babe Ruth. Tris Speaker, Harry Hooper, Larry Gardner, and Duffy Lewis were the hitting stars.

In 1918, the Red Sox decided that Ruth was too good a hitter to be a full-time pitcher. They moved him to the outfield, and he led the league in home runs that season. Ruth also won 13 games on the mound. In 1919, he set a new season record with 29 home runs. That was quite a feat since ballparks were very large and baseballs did not travel as far as they do today.

After the season, Red Sox owner Harry Frazee sold Ruth to the New York Yankees for

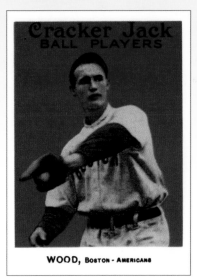

WOOD, Boston - Americans

$100,000. Some believe Frazee decided to use the money to fund a play instead of spending it to improve the team. The play was a success, but Boston started to lose. During the 1920s and 1930s, the Red Sox often finished in last place.

Their luck began to change at the end of the 1930s, when they traded for slugger Jimmie Foxx and pitcher Lefty Grove. A great young hitter named Ted Williams also joined the team. The Red Sox weren't finished. They later added Bobby Doerr, Johnny Pesky, and Dom DiMaggio. Those moves paid off when Boston won the pennant in 1946. Unfortunately, the Red Sox fell in an exciting World Series in seven games.

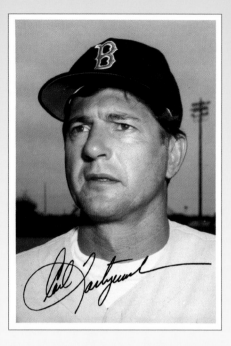

Boston continued to strengthen its roster with more good players, including Ellis Kinder, Mel Parnell, and Jackie Jensen. But the team did not capture another pennant until 1967. That season, the Red Sox won a four-way battle for first place in the AL. They were led by manager Dick Williams and young stars Carl Yastrzemski, Reggie Smith, and Jim Lonborg. Again, Boston lost the World Series in seven games.

In 1975, Yastrzemski was joined by **All-Stars** Carlton Fisk, Jim Rice, Fred Lynn, and Luis Tiant. The Red Sox reached the World Series once more, but again they lost in seven games. Eleven years later, Boston challenged for the championship again. The leaders of that club were Roger Clemens, Wade Boggs, and Rice. The Red Sox advanced to the World Series, where they met the New York Mets.

LEFT: Skinny Ted Williams was nicknamed the "Splendid Splinter."
ABOVE: Carl Yastrzemski was known simply as "Yaz."

The two teams kept fans on the edge of their seats, but the Red Sox lost in—what else?—seven games. Boston fans were heartbroken. Some feared that they would never see their team win the World Series. It would be 18 long years before the Red Sox would get another chance.

In the early years of the 21st century, Boston put together an excellent roster. The team's leading hitters included David Ortiz, Johnny Damon, and Manny Ramirez. Pedro Martinez and Curt Schilling led the pitching staff. In 2003, the Red Sox were just a few outs away from winning the **American League Championship Series (ALCS)** against the Yankees. But New York made an incredible comeback in Game 7 and captured the pennant.

One year later, the teams met again in the ALCS. This time it was Boston that made the amazing comeback. After losing the first three games of the series, the Red Sox battled back to win the next four. In the World Series, they swept the St. Louis Cardinals in four games. For the first time since 1918, the Red Sox were champions. In 2007, they won the World Series again.

In the years between 1918 and 2004, many Boston fans believed that the team's bad luck was punishment for trading Ruth to the Yankees. Some called it the "Curse of the Bambino." Today, after two championships—and the arrival of new stars such as Josh Beckett, Dustin Pedroia, Jacoby Ellsbury, Jon Lester, Carl Crawford, Andrew Bailey, and Adrian Gonzalez—no one is talking about a curse anymore.

LEFT: Manny Ramirez gets a high-five from David Ortiz.
ABOVE: The Red Sox start a wild celebration after winning the 2004 World Series.

HOME TURF

The Red Sox play their home games in Fenway Park. It was built in 1912 and is the oldest stadium in the **big leagues**. Fenway Park has not changed much over the years. A trip there gives you a good idea of how "cozy" ballparks used to be. Some of the stadium's seats are closer to home plate than the dugouts are.

Because Fenway Park was built to fit inside a rectangular city block, the right field and center field fences are far from home plate. The left field fence, on the other hand, is very close. To make it harder to hit home runs, the Red Sox built the wall 37 feet high. It is nicknamed the "Green Monster." A few years ago, the team decided to construct seats on top of the wall. They have become the most popular seats in Fenway Park.

BY THE NUMBERS

- *There are 37,493 seats in Fenway Park.*
- *The distance from home plate to the left field foul pole is 310 feet.*
- *The distance from home plate to the center field fence is 420 feet.*
- *The distance from home plate to the right field foul pole is 302 feet.*

The Red Sox meet the Cleveland Indians in a playoff game at Fenway Park.

Baseball teams in Boston had been wearing red socks long before the Red Sox came to town. The city's NL team, which won several championships during the 1800s, had actually been called the Red Stockings for many years. The Red Sox borrowed their name and then shortened it. Before that, the Red Sox had blue uniforms.

JIMMY FOXX
first base

The first true Red Sox uniform included red socks and a picture of a red sock across the jersey. In the 1930s, the team started featuring a fancy *B* on its cap. The Red Sox also began using the blue-and-red color combination familiar to fans today.

Over the last 70 years, the basic look of the Boston uniform has remained the same. The home jersey has *Red Sox* spelled out in fancy lettering, while the darker road jersey has the name of the city. For special occasions, the team sometimes wears a uniform with either an all-red or all-blue jersey.

LEFT: Jon Lester throws a pitch in the team's 2011 road uniform.
ABOVE: Jimmie Foxx takes a swing for Boston in the late 1930s.

WE WON!

The American League was just two years old in 1903. It had many good teams and players. People wondered which league champion that year—Boston in the AL or the Pittsburgh Pirates in the NL—was the best team in baseball. The owners of the two teams agreed to find out by meeting in a World Series.

The first team to win five games would be crowned the champion of baseball. After losing three of the first four games, Boston won four in a row to win the series. Cy Young and Bill Dineen had all five of the team's victories. Boston's hitting stars were Chick Stahl and Hobe Ferris.

The Red Sox reached the World Series four more times in the early part of the 20th century. They won the championship each time. Boston beat the New York Giants in 1912

LEFT: This scorecard dates back to the 1903 World Series.
RIGHT: Jim Lonborg pitches in the 1967 World Series.

in a close series. The Red Sox had a much easier time against the Philadelphia Phillies in 1915, and also against the Brooklyn Robins in 1916. The Chicago Cubs put up a good fight in 1918, but the Red Sox won in six games.

Boston had many heroes during these years, including Joe Wood, Tris Speaker, Duffy Lewis, Rube Foster, Ernie Shore, Harry Hooper, Carl Mays, and Babe Ruth. In 1918, Ruth pitched and played the outfield for Boston. He won 13 games and also led the AL in home runs. In the World Series, he beat the Cubs twice with great performances on the mound.

The Red Sox had bad luck in their next four trips to the World Series. Each time—1946, 1967, 1975, and 1986—they lost four games to three. These were some of the most exciting World Series ever played. Boston fans were proud of the Red Sox, but after

more than 80 years without a championship, they began to wonder if the team would ever win again.

In 2004, Boston made the **playoffs** as a **Wild Card**. The Red Sox swept through the first round. They lost the first three games of the ALCS to the Yankees. Led by the heavy hitting of David Ortiz, the team fought back to win the next two games in extra innings.

The Red Sox sent Curt Schilling to the mound for the sixth game of the series. Schilling had hurt his ankle in Game 1 and was not expected to play again against the Yankees. He agreed to have a special operation that temporarily fixed the injury, so he could pitch one more time. Schilling quieted the New York bats as his wound oozed blood through his sock. The Red Sox won 4–2 and beat the Yankees again the next night to win the pennant.

The Red Sox faced the St. Louis Cardinals in the World Series. The players felt like no one could beat them now—and they were right!

Boston won four games in a row to win their first championship since 1918. The pitchers were the stars for the Red Sox. Schilling, Pedro Martinez, and Derek Lowe all threw great games.

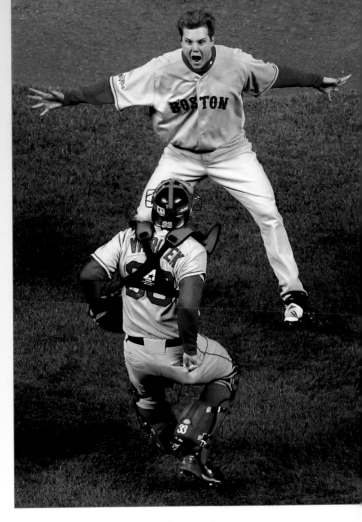

Three years later, the Red Sox returned to the World Series and faced the Colorado Rockies. There were several newcomers on the club, including pitchers Josh Beckett and Jonathan Papelbon, and third baseman Mike Lowell. Beckett won the opening game and the Boston hitters kept the pressure on Colorado for the rest of the series.

As they did in 2004, the Red Sox won four games in a row. Lowell got the winning hit in Game 4 and was named the series **Most Valuable Player (MVP)**. Papelbon was on the mound for the final outs against the Rockies to seal the championship.

LEFT: Curt Schilling yells encouragement to his teammates.
ABOVE: We did it! Jonathan Papelbon gets ready to hug Jason Varitek after Game 4 of the 2007 World Series.

GO-TO GUYS

To be a true star in baseball, you need more than a quick bat and a strong arm. You have to be a "go-to guy"—someone the manager wants on the pitcher's mound or in the batter's box when it matters most. Fans of the Red Sox have had a lot to cheer about over the years, including these great stars …

 ## THE PIONEERS

JIMMIE FOXX   First Baseman

• BORN: 10/22/1907 • DIED: 7/21/1967 • PLAYED FOR TEAM: 1936 TO 1942
Many experts believe that Jimmie Foxx was the best right-handed power hitter in history. He was nicknamed the "Beast." Foxx hit 50 home runs and won the AL batting championship in 1938.

TED WILLIAMS   Outfielder

• BORN: 8/30/1918 • DIED: 7/5/2002
• PLAYED FOR TEAM: 1939 TO 1942 & 1946 TO 1960
Ted Williams understood more about hitting a baseball than any player in history. He won his first batting championship when he was 23 and his sixth when he was 40. Williams was the last player to bat over .400 in a season.

Carl Yastrzemski   Outfielder

- Born: 8/22/1939   • Played for Team: 1961 to 1983

Carl Yastrzemski was Boston's most popular player. At one time or another, he led the AL in hits, runs, doubles, home runs, walks, batting average, and **runs batted in (RBIs)**. In 1967, "Yaz" won the **Triple Crown** and led the Red Sox to the pennant.

Jim Rice   Outfielder

- Born: 3/8/1953

- Played for Team: 1974 to 1989

No one in baseball hit the ball harder than Jim Rice. His best season came in 1978, when he was named AL MVP. That year, he became the only player ever to lead the big leagues in home runs, triples, and RBIs in the same season.

Carlton Fisk   Catcher

- Born: 12/26/1947

- Played for Team: 1969 to 1980

Carlton Fisk was one of the most valuable players in baseball during the 1970s. He controlled the pace of games as a catcher and was an excellent hitter. His 12th-inning home run in Game 6 of the 1975 World Series is one of baseball's most famous moments.

RIGHT: Jim Rice

WADE BOGGS   Third Baseman

• BORN: 6/15/1958   • PLAYED FOR TEAM: 1982 TO 1992

Wade Boggs was a hitting machine. From 1983 to 1988, he won five batting championships. Pitchers hated to throw Boggs a strike—he received the most **intentional walks** in the league six years in a row.

ROGER CLEMENS   Pitcher

• BORN: 8/4/1962   • PLAYED FOR TEAM: 1984 TO 1996

Roger Clemens had three different fastballs and two different **breaking balls**—and he threw them all hard. The "Rocket" won the AL MVP in 1986 and the **Cy Young Award** three times while pitching for Boston.

PEDRO MARTINEZ   Pitcher

• BORN: 10/25/1971   • PLAYED FOR TEAM: 1998 TO 2004

Pedro Martinez was a magician with the baseball. He could throw any pitch at any speed to any part of the strike zone. Martinez won the Cy Young Award twice with Boston.

MANNY RAMIREZ   Outfielder

• BORN: 5/30/1972   • PLAYED FOR TEAM: 2001 TO 2008

Manny Ramirez was the league's top right-handed hitter during his time with the Red Sox. He won the batting championship in 2002 and led the AL in homers in 2004.

DAVID ORTIZ — Designated Hitter

- BORN: 11/18/1975   • FIRST YEAR WITH TEAM: 2003

No one has more fun playing baseball than David Ortiz. In 2004, his leadership helped the Red Sox win the World Series. After that, Ortiz led the league in RBIs in 2005 and set a team record with 54 home runs in 2006.

DUSTIN PEDROIA — Second Baseman

- BORN: 8/17/1983
- FIRST YEAR WITH TEAM: 2006

Dustin Pedroia proved that a little guy could succeed in the big leagues. He was named **Rookie of the Year** in 2007 and MVP the following season. Pedroia led the AL in runs scored two years in a row.

ADRIAN GONZALEZ — First Baseman

- BORN: 5/8/1982
- FIRST YEAR WITH TEAM: 2011

The Red Sox traded four of their best young players to get Adrian Gonzalez. In his first season in Boston, he led the AL in hits and had the highest batting average on the team. Fans nicknamed him "A-Gone" for his long home runs.

LEFT: Pedro Martinez   **ABOVE**: Adrian Gonzalez

23

CALLING THE SHOTS

Baseball managers face incredible pressure. They are expected to lead their team to victory every game. In the years between Boston's championships in 1918 and 2004, the managers of the Red Sox were under more pressure than anyone. During that time, the city's hockey, basketball, and football teams all won championships. With each passing season, Boston baseball fans grew more impatient. When the Red Sox fell short, the manager usually took the blame.

During those years, Boston had some fine managers. Joe Cronin led the club for 13 seasons. For six of those seasons, he was a **player-manager**. The Red Sox finished second in the AL four times and won one pennant under Cronin, in 1946. That season, they lost to the St. Louis Cardinals in a thrilling World Series.

Dick Williams, Darrell Johnson, and John McNamara each led the Red Sox to the pennant, too. Williams made a young team believe in itself in 1967. He taught his players to do all the little things right. Boston went from ninth place to first place in one year. Johnson managed the Red Sox to the World Series in 1975. Unlike

Terry Francona managed Boston to two World Series championships.

the energetic Williams, Johnson was always very calm. He rarely took chances because he had so many talented players. McNamara was the same way. His 1986 Red Sox knew how to handle almost any situation.

The manager who finally won it all in Boston was Terry Francona. He did not have many rules. He put the responsibility on his players to get ready for every game. If there was a problem in the locker room, Francona stayed out of it. He spent most of his time preparing for games. He rarely made a mistake once the action started.

Under Francona, the Red Sox won the pennant in 2004 and 2007. In both years, they went on to win the World Series. Francona enjoyed the pressure of managing the Red Sox. And after all those years of frustration in Boston, it felt great to bring a championship to Red Sox fans.

ONE GREAT DAY

Ted Williams was baseball's most confident hitter. Every time he walked to the plate, he believed he would win his battle with the pitcher. In 1941, Williams had a magical season. Yet, for most of the year, no one noticed that his average was over .400. Joe DiMaggio of the New York Yankees was making headlines as he got at least one hit in 56 games in a row. Only later that summer did fans realize Williams had a chance to make history, too.

Ten seasons had passed since anyone had batted .400 for an entire year. Entering the final day of the 1941 season, Williams was batting .39955. If he didn't play, the league would round up his average to .400 for the season. If he played, he risked seeing his average drop. Boston manager Joe Cronin asked Williams what he wanted to do. "I'm not going to do it sitting on the bench," he told Cronin.

The Red Sox were set to meet the Philadelphia Athletics in a doubleheader. In the first game, Williams drilled a single his first time up, and later hit a home run. He finished the contest with four hits.

Ted Williams crosses the plate after a home run in the 1941 All-Star Game. It was a magical season for the "Splendid Splinter."

Williams played in the second game, even though it was difficult to see the ball in the fall shadows. After getting a single, he hit a pitch in the fourth inning harder than any in his career. The ball went through the infield on a low line and continued straight to the outfield fence. It hit a speaker and bounced back on the field for a double.

At the end of the day, Williams had six hits in eight trips to the plate. He finished the season batting .406. As all those experts predicted, no one has hit .400 since.

LEGEND HAS IT

LEGEND HAS IT that Wade Boggs was. Like many baseball players, Boggs was *superstitious*. When he was hitting well, he did not like to change anything he did before a game. That included eating chicken. Boggs started doing this every day as a rookie and hit .349. After that season, he never stopped. Boggs hit better than .300 for the next nine seasons. To keep from getting bored with chicken, he began trying different recipes. Boggs ended up with so many that he wrote a cookbook called *Fowl Tips*.

ABOVE: Wade Boggs believed that a pregame meal of chicken helped him hit better.

LEGEND HAS IT that it was number 337. One spring in the early 1970s, pitcher Bill Lee asked if he could change his number from 37 to 337. This was not the first unusual thing he had done. In fact, Lee was nicknamed the "Spaceman" because sometimes he acted as if he were on another planet. In this case, however, he had a perfectly good reason for the odd request—when you turn 337 upside down, it spells "LEE."

WHICH BOSTON PLAYER TIED A RECORD SHARED BY BABE RUTH AND CY YOUNG?

LEGEND HAS IT that Daisuke Matsuzaka did. Matsuzaka started Game 3 of the 2007 World Series for the Red Sox. In the third inning, he came to bat with the bases loaded. Matsuzaka singled to left field to score Mike Lowell and Jason Varitek. Before that, Ruth and Young had been the only Red Sox pitchers to drive in two runs in a World Series game. Along the way, Matsuzaka also became the first Japanese pitcher to start and win a game in the World Series.

The Red Sox lost the 1975 World Series to the Cincinnati Reds four games to three. But you would never know it talking to Boston fans. They still rave about Game 6 of that series—one of the most exciting **postseason** games ever played.

The Reds held the lead, three games to two. When the series moved from Cincinnati to Boston, rain delayed the sixth game for four days. The long wait added to the drama of the game. A record 70 million fans tuned in to watch it on television.

The Red Sox took a 3–0 lead on a home run by Fred Lynn, but the Reds tied it up. Cincinnati scored three more times to take a 6–3 lead. With two outs in the eighth inning, the Red Sox sent pinch-hitter Bernie Carbo up to bat. He cracked a long home run with two runners on base to tie the game.

The Red Sox loaded the bases in the next inning, but George Foster made a perfect throw from left field to keep the winning run from scoring. In the 11th inning, Cincinnati's Joe Morgan hit a ball toward the seats in right field. Dwight Evans caught it before it went over the fence. Who would the next hero be?

Carlton Fisk leaps into the air after his home run sails out of the park.

His name was Carlton Fisk, and he was one of Boston's most beloved players. Fisk was the **leadoff batter** in the bottom of the 12th inning. He swung hard at the first pitch he saw and sent a long, curving drive down the left field line. Everyone in Fenway Park held their breath. Would the ball go foul? Fisk tried to "help" it stay fair by waving his arms. When the ball curled into the foul pole, he jumped for joy. It was a game-winning home run!

REDSOX
MAGIC NUMBER
0 OUTS
TO END THE CURSE

TEAM SPIRIT

Some people in New England say that the most valuable thing you can own is **season tickets** to the Red Sox. They're not kidding! Fenway Park is sold out year after year. Fans with good seats can sell their tickets for several times what they paid for them. Fans have been known to do some crazy things to get their hands on a pair of tickets near the field.

In 2003, the Red Sox added 274 seats atop the left field wall. They weren't sure if fans would like these seats because they were very far away from the action. The Green Monster seating section became an instant hit. Some fans would rather sit there than behind home plate!

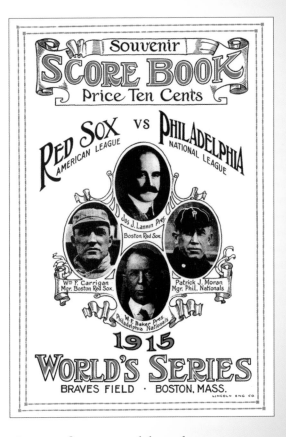

LEFT: Fans in 2004 celebrate the end of the Curse of the Bambino.
ABOVE: Fans in 1915 watched the Red Sox play in the World Series.

TIMELINE

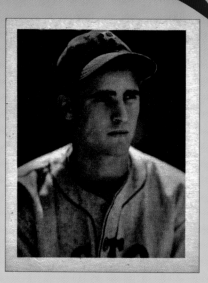

Bobby Doerr batted .409 in the 1946 World Series.

1903
Boston wins the first modern World Series.

1946
The Red Sox win the AL pennant.

1918
The Red Sox win their fifth World Series.

1941
Ted Williams bats .406.

1960
Ted Williams homers in the last trip to the plate of his career.

Out on fly.

BUCK FREEMAN
BOSTON.

Buck Freeman led the 1903 team in home runs.

Ted Williams is congratulated after the final home run of his career.

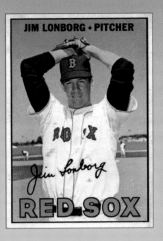

Jim Lonborg won 22 games in 1967.

Roger Clemens

1967
The Red Sox win the pennant.

2004
The Red Sox win their first World Series since 1918.

2007
The Red Sox win the World Series again.

1986
Roger Clemens strikes out 20 Seattle Mariners in a game.

2011
Jacoby Ellsbury is the first Boston player with 30 homers and 30 steals in the same season.

Mike Lowell was named 2007 World Series MVP.

FUN FACTS

BOSTON SPEED PARTY
Dustin Pedroia • Jacoby Ellsbury

ONE-TWO PUNCH

Jacoby Ellsbury and Dustin Pedroia batted first and second for the Red Sox in 2007. They were the first rookies ever to hit "one-two" for a World Series champion.

FLYING HIGH

Ted Williams missed all or part of five seasons during **World War II** and the **Korean War**. With his quick reflexes and excellent eyesight, he was one of America's best fighter pilots.

LOAFING AROUND

Carl Yastrzemski was such a hero to the kids of New England that he had his own brand of white bread: Yaz Bread.

ABOVE: A trading card shows teammates Dustin Pedroia and Jacoby Ellsbury.   **RIGHT**: Fred Lynn watches a hit during his amazing rookie season.

The Kid Can Hit

In 1965, Boston outfielder Tony Conigliaro led the AL in home runs. At the age of 20, he was the youngest player in league history to do so.

Young Leader

In 1975, Fred Lynn had the greatest year of any Boston rookie. He batted .331, led the AL in runs and doubles, and helped the Red Sox reach the World Series. After the season, Lynn became the first player ever to be named Rookie of the Year and MVP in the same season.

First in Fielding

In 2008, Kevin Youkilis broke the all-time record for first basemen when he played his 195th game in a row without an error. His streak lasted 238 games.

Fast Start

In 2011, Jonathan Papelbon became the first pitcher to **save** 30 or more games in each of his first six full seasons. He reached 200 saves faster than any pitcher in history.

TALKING BASEBALL

"My whole time in Boston, I gave everything I could—everything I knew I was about—on and off the field."

▶ *NOMAR GARCIAPARRA, ON HIS DEVOTION TO THE RED SOX*

"There's only one way to become a hitter. Go up to the plate and get mad. Get mad at yourself and mad at the pitcher."

▶ *TED WILLIAMS, ON THE MENTAL APPROACH TO HITTING*

"I think about baseball when I wake up in the morning. I think about it all day and I dream about it at night."

▶ *CARL YASTRZEMSKI, ON HIS LOVE OF THE GAME*

"When you win, you eat better and sleep better."

▶ **JOHNNY PESKY**, ON THE BENEFITS OF PLAYING ON A WINNING TEAM

"I just love the feeling from the fans. That puts you into the game more than anything."

▶ **DAVID ORTIZ**, ON THE CROWD'S ENERGY AT FENWAY PARK

"There are no days off in the **AL East**."

▶ **JOSH BECKETT**, ON PLAYING AGAINST STIFF COMPETITION

"Whenever I hit a ball in the gap, I'm thinking extra bases. I never slow down. "

▶ **CARL CRAWFORD**, ON HOW HE HITS SO MANY TRIPLES

LEFT: Nomar Garciaparra   **ABOVE**: David Ortiz

GREAT DEBATES

People who root for the Red Sox love to compare their favorite moments, teams, and players. Some debates have been going on for years! How would you settle these classic baseball arguments?

MOVING REGGIE SMITH TO CENTER FIELD WAS THE SMARTEST POSITION CHANGE THE RED SOX EVER MADE …

… because it helped them win the pennant. Smith began the 1967 season at second base. After a week, Dick Williams moved him to center field to replace light-hitting Jose Tartabull. Meanwhile, Mike Andrews took over at second. Smith played great defense and finished second in the voting for Rookie of the Year. Andrews was one of the top hitters at his position in 1967.

SORRY, MOVING KEVIN YOUKILIS TO FIRST BASE WAS EVEN SMARTER …

… because it helped the Red Sox win the pennant and the World Series. "Youk" (LEFT) was a third baseman up until 2006. That season, Terry Francona asked him to play first base. The move created an opening for Mike Lowell. By 2007, Youkilis was the top-fielding first baseman in baseball. Lowell drove in 120 runs in 2007 and was the MVP of the World Series.

... because he was an All-Star shortstop five times for the Red Sox. Cronin was a regular at the position for seven years in the 1930s. After that he served as a third baseman, first baseman, and pinch-hitter. All the while, he managed the club. Cronin batted exactly .300 for the Red Sox. Although he didn't win a pennant as a player-manager, he did lead Boston to the AL crown as a manager the first season after he retired.

NOT SO FAST. TAKE A LOOK AT JIMMY COLLINS ...

... because he led the team to two pennants and victory in the World Series. Collins (RIGHT) was Boston's manager during its first six seasons, from 1901 to 1906. For most of that time, he was also the best third baseman in the game. Collins batted over .300 twice and was a magician on defense. No one was better at fielding grounders and bunts. Collins was a speedy runner, too. He stole three bases in the 1903 World Series to help Boston win its first championship.

Ball.

JIMMY COLLINS
BOSTON.

FOR THE RECORD

The great Red Sox teams and players have left their marks on the record books. These are the "best of the best" …

Carlton Fisk

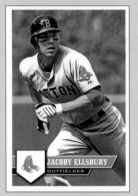

Jacoby Ellsbury

RED SOX AWARD WINNERS

WINNER	AWARD	YEAR
Jimmie Foxx	Most Valuable Player	1938
Ted Williams	Most Valuable Player	1946
Ted Williams	Most Valuable Player	1949
Walt Dropo	Rookie of the Year	1950
Jackie Jensen	Most Valuable Player	1958
Don Schwall	Rookie of the Year	1961
Carl Yastrzemski	Most Valuable Player	1967
Jim Lonborg	Cy Young Award	1967
Carlton Fisk	Rookie of the Year	1972
Fred Lynn	Rookie of the Year	1975
Fred Lynn	Most Valuable Player	1975
Jim Rice	Most Valuable Player	1978
Roger Clemens	Most Valuable Player	1986
Roger Clemens	Cy Young Award	1986
John McNamara	Manager of the Year	1986
Roger Clemens	Cy Young Award	1987
Roger Clemens	Cy Young Award	1991
Mo Vaughn	Most Valuable Player	1995
Nomar Garciaparra	Rookie of the Year	1997
Pedro Martinez	Cy Young Award	1999
Jimy Williams	Manager of the Year	1999
Pedro Martinez	Cy Young Award	2000
Manny Ramirez	World Series MVP	2004
Dustin Pedroia	Rookie of the Year	2007
Mike Lowell	World Series MVP	2007
Dustin Pedroia	Most Valuable Player	2008
Jacoby Ellsbury	Comeback Player of the Year	2011

RED SOX ACHIEVEMENTS

ACHIEVEMENT	YEAR
AL Pennant Winners	1903
World Series Champions	1903
AL Pennant Winners	1904
AL Pennant Winners	1912
World Series Champions	1912
AL Pennant Winners	1915
World Series Champions	1915
AL Pennant Winners	1916
World Series Champions	1916
AL Pennant Winners	1918
World Series Champions	1918
AL Pennant Winners	1946
AL Pennant Winners	1967
AL East Champions	1975
AL Pennant Winners	1975
AL East Champions	1986
AL Pennant Winners	1986
AL East Champions	1988
AL East Champions	1990
AL East Champions	1995
AL Pennant Winners	2004
World Series Champions	2004
AL East Champions	2007
AL Pennant Winners	2007
World Series Champions	2007

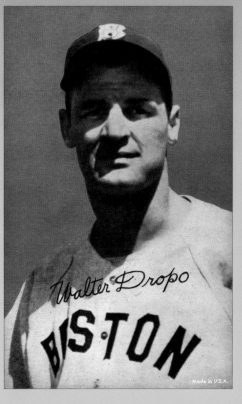

ABOVE: Walt Dropo
BELOW: Kevin Millar and Johnny Damon were key members of the 2004 team.

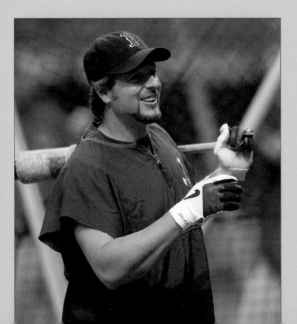

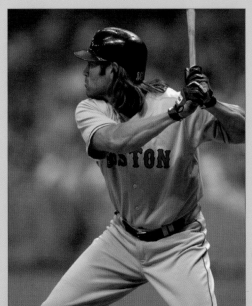

PINPOINTS

The history of a baseball team is made up of many smaller stories. These stories take place all over the map—not just in the city a team calls "home." Match the pushpins on these maps to the **TEAM FACTS**, and you will begin to see the story of the Red Sox unfold!

TEAM FACTS

1 Boston, Massachusetts—*The Red Sox have played here since 1901.*

2 Bellows Falls, Vermont—*Carlton Fisk was born here.*

3 Anderson, South Carolina—*Jim Rice was born here.*

4 Hubbard, Texas—*Tris Speaker was born here.*

5 St. Louis, Missouri—*The Red Sox won the 2004 World Series here.*

6 Aberdeen, South Dakota—*Terry Francona was born here.*

7 San Diego, California—*Ted Williams was born here.*

8 Denver, Colorado—*The Red Sox won the 2007 World Series here.*

9 Anchorage, Alaska—*Curt Schilling was born here.*

10 Tokyo, Japan—*Daisuke Matsuzaka was born here.*

11 Marianao, Cuba—*Luis Tiant was born here.*

12 Santo Domingo, Dominican Republic—*Manny Ramirez was born here.*

Luis Tiant

GLOSSARY

AL EAST—A group of American League teams that play in the eastern part of the country.

ALL-STARS—Players who are selected to play in baseball's annual All-Star Game.

AMERICAN LEAGUE (AL)—One of baseball's two major leagues; the AL began play in 1901.

AMERICAN LEAGUE CHAMPIONSHIP SERIES (ALCS)—The playoff series that has decided the American League pennant since 1969.

BIG LEAGUES—The top level of professional baseball.

BREAKING BALLS—Pitches that move as they near home plate, such as curveballs, sliders, or sinkers.

CY YOUNG AWARD—The award given each year to each league's best pitcher.

INTENTIONAL WALKS—A statistic that measures the number of times a batter is walked on purpose.

KOREAN WAR—The war between North Korea and South Korea that lasted from 1950 to 1953. The United States fought on the South Korean side.

LEADOFF BATTER—The first hitter in a lineup, or the first hitter in an inning.

MOST VALUABLE PLAYER (MVP)—The award given each year to each league's top player; an MVP is also selected for the World Series and the All-Star Game.

NATIONAL LEAGUE (NL)—The older of the two major leagues; the NL began play in 1876.

PENNANT—A league championship. The term comes from the triangular flag awarded to each season's champion, beginning in the 1870s.

PLAYER-MANAGER—A player who also manages his team.

PLAYOFFS—The games played after the regular season to determine which teams will advance to the World Series.

POSTSEASON—The games played after the regular season, including the playoffs and World Series.

ROOKIE OF THE YEAR—The annual award given to each league's best first-year player.

RUNS BATTED IN (RBIS)—A statistic that counts the number of runners a batter drives home.

SAVE—Record the last out or outs in a team's win. A relief pitcher on the mound at the end of a close victory is credited with a "save."

SEASON TICKETS—A package of tickets to every home game.

SUPERSTITIOUS—Trusting in magic or luck.

TRADITION—A belief or custom that is handed down from generation to generation.

TRIPLE CROWN—An honor given to a player who leads the league in home runs, batting average, and RBIs.

WILD CARD—A playoff spot reserved for a team that does not win its division, but finishes with a good record.

WORLD SERIES—The world championship series played between the AL and NL pennant winners.

WORLD WAR II—The war between the major powers of Europe, Asia, and North America that lasted from 1939 to 1945. The United States entered the war in 1941.

Extra Innings

TEAM SPIRIT introduces a great way to stay up to date with your team! Visit our **EXTRA INNINGS** link and get connected to the latest and greatest updates. **EXTRA INNINGS** serves as a young reader's ticket to an exclusive web page—with more stories, fun facts, team records, and photos of the Red Sox. Content is updated during and after each season. The **EXTRA INNINGS** feature also enables readers to send comments and letters to the author! Log onto:

www.norwoodhousepress.com/library.aspx

and click on the tab: TEAM SPIRIT to access **EXTRA INNINGS**.

Read all the books in the series to learn more about professional sports. For a complete listing of the baseball, basketball, football, and hockey teams in the TEAM SPIRIT series, visit our website at:

www.norwoodhousepress.com/library.aspx

ON THE ROAD

BOSTON RED SOX
4 Yawkey Way
Boston, Massachusetts 02215
(617) 226-6000
boston.redsox.mlb.com

**NATIONAL BASEBALL
HALL OF FAME AND MUSEUM**
25 Main Street
Cooperstown, New York 13326
(888) 425-5633
www.baseballhalloffame.org

ON THE BOOKSHELF

To learn more about the sport of baseball, look for these books at your library or bookstore:

* Augustyn, Adam (editor). *The Britannica Guide to Baseball*. New York, NY: Rosen Publishing, 2011.

* Dreier, David. *Baseball: How It Works*. North Mankato, MN: Capstone Press, 2010.

* Stewart, Mark. *Ultimate 10: Baseball*. New York, NY: Gareth Stevens Publishing, 2009.

INDEX

PAGE NUMBERS IN **BOLD** REFER TO ILLUSTRATIONS.

ABOUT THE AUTHOR

MARK STEWART has written more than 50 books on baseball and over 150 sports books for kids. He grew up in New York City during the 1960s rooting for the Yankees and Mets, and was lucky enough to meet players from both teams. Mark comes from a family of writers. His grandfather was Sunday Editor of *The New York Times,* and his mother was Articles Editor of *Ladies' Home Journal* and *McCall's*. Mark has profiled hundreds of athletes over the past 25 years. He has also written several books about his native New York and New Jersey, his home today. Mark is a graduate of Duke University, with a degree in history. He lives and works in a home overlooking Sandy Hook, New Jersey. You can contact Mark through the Norwood House Press website.